THE ART OF THOUGHTS

POETRY, PROSE, QUOTES, AND WORDS

PAUL HER

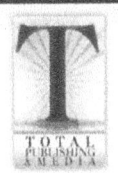

www.TotalPublishingAndMedia.com

Copyright © 2015, Paul Her

All rights reserved.

No part of this book may be reproduced, stored in a retrieval system, or transmitted by any means, electronic, mechanical, photocopying, recording, or otherwise, without written permission from the author.

ISBN 978-1-63302-032-0
eISBN 978-1-63302-033-7

FOREWORD

I am excited! The world should be excited too, because Paul Her has written another book of poetry, and this one is even more amazing. Paul is a wordsmith whose observations and values shine through his work. Each poem in this collection is one that comes from his heart, and the words tell stories of everyday topics in which we can all relate. That's the charm of a book of poetry by Paul Her – it's always going to be comforting, witty, and thoughtful. As a therapist, I frequently use poetry, metaphor, and prose to teach my clients. This helps them to articulate feelings and learn new truths about the world and themselves. Paul's book will make my job easier. But this book is not just for therapists to share, it is for all of us. There is wisdom in the poetry, a call for justice and a balance to living life that can only be a product of his triumph over challenges few of us will ever face. My favorite part of reading one of Paul's books of poetry is the sense of peace I receive, and the reassurance that excellent art is still being made. Some people will tell you that poetry is a dying art form – all one needs to do is to pick up a copy of any of Paul's wonderful collections to know that isn't true.

Dr. Richard Nongard
Author of Transformational Leadership: How To Lead From Your Strengths And Maximize Your Impact

DEDICATION

With sincere dedication to my wife, Jayleena Yang Her. Thank you for your inspiration in molding me into a better husband. Her patience toward me is deeply appreciated. Furthermore, she contributes ideas and words to two poems (*She is Broken* and *Selfish Hearts*). It is written from her views and with my editing, the poems became two of my favorites. Moreover, the poem *A Poem from a Girl* is also from a concept of another friend. This friend knows who she is and I am grateful to publish the work we did together.

My second dedication is for my dear cousins in Canada. They have shown me brotherly love throughout my life. My cousins are more like brothers: Chue Fue Heu, Davit Heu, Paul Heu, France Heu, Marc Heu, and Johner Heu. I will not forget your kindness. Without you guys, I would not be as thoughtful as I am today. My experience in Canada will live with me for the rest of my life.

As my final dedication, I want to thank my good friend, Dr. Richard Nongard, for his kind and wonderful words. I admire your intelligence and wisdom. I enjoy reading your books and am learning to be a far better thinker because of your writings. For your time and effort, for reading this project and submitting a *Foreword* for me, and for your great support, I will be forever grateful and humble.

Acknowledgment

I would like to acknowledge two federally funded programs that have impacted my life. The first one is the Upward Bound Program (Michigan State University, East Lansing, MI). This program is coordinated by two of the most wonderful people I have met in my path: Sandra T. Firestone and Glenda Hammond. I am grateful to have known you both. You are the silencers which speak louder than any roar of a thunder. You both have impacted many lives and not taken any credit for it, but you perform your job with passion to improve the well-being of minority students. With class and pure intentions, you both have changed my life and many lives to have higher standards with education, and with great gratitude, I thank you both from the bottom of my heart.

The second program is the Ronald E. McNair Program (Siena Heights University, Adrian, MI). Without the support of this program, my eyes would not have been opened beyond the undergraduate level of education. Although I am short of my commitment to this program, which is to pursue a Doctorate, my dream is still alive. I will try my best to be a scholar again in the near future. The experiences I have gained from this program showed me how to be a professional in every area I have pursued.

From The Publisher

You hold in your hands a great buffet of words. I use the food analogy because besides being a great motivator, educator and poet, Paul Her is a successful restaurateur. The food at his eatery is always delicious; the menu displaying a wide variety of choices. The buffet you hold in your hands has within it an extensive offering of thoughts, ideas, and feelings. Just as you would not attempt to devour the full menu of a restaurant in one sitting, enjoy each poem, one at a time, as a tasty dish which stands alone. Think of each line or thought as a nourishing bite. Eat (read) until you are conformable; dessert is just a page turn away.

Contents

The Struggle is Real 1
My Aqua Imprisonment 3
A Message to My Friends 4
Transitional Love 6
Travel Through the Night 7
Lost in Life 8
Process of Change 9
Judgment Day Before Inferno 10
A Disguise of Excellency 11
A Distinctive Rose 13
Unbroken Hope 14
Do Not Fall for Me 15
When You Are Lost 16
A Poem from a Girl 17
Wrongful Love 19
She Is Broken 20
The Deceitful Followers 21
It Was a Simpler Time 23
My Dear Cousin 26
She is My Beautiful 27
The Movie of My Life 28

Title	Page
A Night Visionary	29
Oh, Mr. Gatsby	30
Gone, but not Forgotten	31
Selfish Hearts	32
Incarceration	33
Greed of Humanity	34
My Closest Friends	36
Dearest…	37
My Unborn Child	38
Inner Strength of David	39
A Passage in My Mind	40
O Darlin' Night	41
Seasons	42
A United Family	43
A Wishful Want	44
Any Given Day	46
Hmoob Caubfab (Hmong in the Jungle)	47
To My Amicable Hmong Women	49
Love and Justice	50
Hurting Inside Me	51
Who Do We Blame?	52
Broken Dreams	53
I Am Free (My Soul)	54
A Secret Garden	55

Mishap of Time	57
When I Am Gone	58
Hate Hinders	59
Lion's Entrapment	60
The Concept of Good	61
Along the Roads	63
Her Cry for Help	65
A Mother's Love	66
An Introduction into My Perspectives	67
Words for Thoughts	69
Quotes for Insights	71
A Simple Truth	72
Views on Isolation	73
Views on Mindfulness	74
Views on Measurement of Life	75
Being Afraid	76
Quotes on Self-Happiness	77
Quotes on the Possession of Power	78
Quotes on the Measure of Success	79
Quotes on Being a Leader	80
Words for Improvement	82
Believe in Yourself	83
Words for the Heart	84
Words for the Mind	85

The Mind is Our Freedom 86
Death Ceremony in the Hmong Community... 87
Words for Inspiration 89
Be an Achiever in Life 90
Words to Remember... 91
For the Love Birds 93

The Struggle is Real

The struggle is real
The pain may be temporary
Let me paint a picture of the social problems
Through the expression of contemporary literature
Through the blinded eyes of the rich
And their powerful masters

The struggle is here
The pain is real
They say the poor are lazy,
Even viewed as crazy
The system is a vicious cycle
A structure invented to suffer
Those who are already suffering

The struggle is real
The pain will not disappear
The politicians cannot agree; they don't care
They just say the words we want to hear
All they want is for those seats to be there –
Secure for their better years

The struggle is here
The pain creates fear
All of us are not a success, but a waste of time
Desperate for money and fame,
Materialism and a respectable name

Paul Her

The struggle is real
The pain is real
We as people need to let go of our egos
We have to swallow our pride,
Let's not act on false principles
But on the holy morality of man,
And with hope
We can redeem the sins of humble humanity
From this evolution called MAN

MY AQUA IMPRISONMENT

I am frozen in amazement.
Staring into this trapped aqua-haven
Of an unnatural habitat, but fascinating;
I am lost in awe,
Confined in my constructed tropical paradise;
Beautiful creatures swim endlessly,
Brushing their colorful gills against the steady fluid
With pure innocence of the naïve unknown.
They do not know their purpose,
But I am sure of my selfish reason.
They are not to be disturbed as they
Are in their comfortable environment.
If only they knew they are my drug;
Soon to be imprisoned in eternity for the
Enjoyment of my therapeutic session.
This tropical creation could soothe
The depressed soul of any man.
It will relieve the mind of unwanted
Thoughts and free the eyes of gruesome images.
To forsake the evil in this wicked world.
It will be my therapy –
To indulge in this peaceful display of endless tranquility.

Paul Her

A Message to My Friends

Be in the presence of friends,
Cherish the company of laughter.
Stay still in this moment of joy,
Act faithfully to the given bond of love.

Refresh the will to reach higher,
Join together to limit self-pride.
Don't pretend to be something you're not,
But begin to be truthful as one.

Open to the judgment of others,
As if you are letting go of disgrace.
Stop creeping like the lions under the grass;
Come forth together in a circle to dance.

Be free into the winds of unknown,
Feel the freedom of Democracy.
Stay wise to popular news of the media,
Not all can be true and comforting.

You keep complaining about the actions of others,
But you don't change your own actions.
Why worry so much about them?
Change the things you wish to become.

Fill your cup tastefully with fate,
Drink to the beauty of life's mystery.

The Art of Thoughts

Why resort to the petite life?
When you can have a castle.

We should not hiss evilly like a snake,
Rather, we should flock proudly like a pack of ducks.
Think of thoughtless portraits of love,
Pay it forward for humanity's soul.

If you have the choice to live freely,
Why do you find a way to be behind bars?
Live the life you don't regret,
Find the purpose of your own journey.

Paul Her

Transitional Love

I tried to conquer
And I failed miserably
But, I've forgotten

I kept moving forward
No matter how painful the battles
Oh, I *will* keep fighting

I cannot settle for less
This life is deceiving
However, I won't fall down

I will lose you
I will move on
But, it'll never be the same

Travel Through the Night

O beloved friends of guilty beings
Let's begin this night to travel
Through the dark without the sun

Mark my words, there is no time for rested ambition
Open your eyes to observe
See the stars; do not sleep with the dreamers

Breathe the windy air of this night
The fresh air is not here to stay
We will travel, anxiously awaiting for arrival

Through the darkness we will not see as we
Ask for safe travel from the Guardian Angels
Follow the light of the stars beneath the wide sky,
O lovers of the quiet night.
Cease for a moment to listen and hear the sound
Of the drums played by the harmonious Moon

My dear friends, let's be true friends
And be as silent as the night
Listen to our hearts –
We shall become one with fate

Paul Her

LOST IN LIFE

I sat and observed the cycle of life
Each is consumed without knowing,
Not aware of – In robotic mode
Like a line of ants,
Feasting on life's leftovers.

Only bicker to worsen the spirit
No comprehension –
No compassion –
No longer considerate, emotionless, numb feelings
Living just to pass the time.

Where is the human love?
Why be strangers in the union of friendships?
Interact with passion
Learn from the violent histories
If not, we could destroy humanity

Think to improve your worth
Know – you are not the product of waste
Value the conversations from others
Realistic extinction of human noises is devastating
Don't be the one to pile the problems

Live to cherish life's worst personality
The best of us can be lost in life
Remember to smell the wild flowers along the trenches

Halt to view the dying garden
Even you can disappear without knowing

Process of Change

Do you know what it takes to make it?
Do you see your mistakes when you have lost the debates?
It is a shame some of you think I don't deserve to be where I am!
You even think I am lucky; perhaps I am lucky, maybe even blessed.
But the truth is I worked my freaking ass OFF.
Don't envy me or hate me.
Get to know me; sit down, let's have a conservation.
Each drink a cup of tea.
Take a walk with me side by side; know my story, and feel my struggles.
Understand – If you were to set foot in other people's shoes,
You may not survive their journey.
Can you figure out your purpose before your time is up?
Will you give up when the times are tough?
Learn to live your life instead of living vicariously through others.
If you have the time to judge others,
You can make the time to better yourself.
Be you and never regret your own life.

Paul Her

JUDGMENT DAY BEFORE INFERNO

If you are to judge me based on the thoughts of my mind,
I will be destined to enter the gate of the Inferno.
If you are to conclude on the kind gestures I have done,
I will be a Saint waiting to be canonized in His Kingdom.
I want to assure you; do not cast your final judgment on me
Until you can know the reasons behind my actions.
I am far from salvation, but I have repented for forgiveness
I am not purely innocent, but my conscience knows the righteous morals.
What separates me from a killer is the ability to escape the world created by our minds,
I have a guilty conscience, and he abided by the law of his wicked conscience.
My thoughts are no different from a killer, my mind is not different,
The only difference is my action, my understanding of right from wrong.
I am nothing special, in fact I am not better than any murderer,
I just happen to know how to differentiate reality
From the premeditated fantasy of my mind.

A Disguise of Excellency

A sweet tenderloin taste of quality
Melts like the ice on a warm day in the city

A treat that fills your soul to the limits
Satisfies your cravings with a perfect image

Simmering timelessly until a delightful taste
To last forever in memories not to be erased

A masterpiece of art and heavenly smell
A cuisine relentlessly curing all the ills

A Distinctive Rose

A rose – so peaceful and discrete
So powerless, but never surrenders to defeat
She is the envy of all men
But joy and happiness to all women
Perfection with pure devotion
Exists to cure the emotions of all occasions
She comes in all colors without any intent for attraction
But it's only with her presence
That can release the condolences of the nation
Her aroma is a smell of diluted contradictions
For only she is a true master of remarkable illusions
A rose – so beautiful and complete
So lifeless, but so full of distinctive mystique

Paul Her

UNBROKEN HOPE

There's a lonely place that I don't want anyone of you to go
It's a place I wish for no one to know
I can feel the emptiness of lost hope
I can see the bitterness of a fiend without a shot of dope

Don't listen to the lies of these pretentious pricks of scam
Their hearts will not be pure so let them be damned
I cannot allow you to feel the suffocation of misery
I would not recommend the repeat of a gruesome history

In a place where no one should belong
Even if you deserve it for what you have done wrong
I don't wish for any person to experience inferno
I hope for a brighter day tomorrow

Let the angel of love kiss away our broken sorrows
Let Him give us wings to fly freely like innocent sparrows

Do Not Fall for Me

Do not fall for me because I am charming and elegant
Do not fall for me because I say the words you want to hear
Fall for me because I am falling for you

Do not fall for me because I buy you flowers on special occasions
Do not fall for me because I take you to nice places
Fall for me because I cannot wait to take you home to meet my parents

Do not fall for me because I am a smooth talker
Do not fall for me because I am lovable and funny
Fall for me because I will stay true by your side

Do not fall for me because I have an inviting smile
Do not fall for me because I can give you sweet kisses
Fall for me because I am faithful to you

Do not fall for me because I am romantic and caring
Do not fall for me because I offer you security
Fall for me because I cannot live without you

Paul Her

When You Are Lost

When you are lost in between two worlds
A part of you wants to stay
But a part of you wants to let go
When you are lost in your own ways
The memories of the past won't stray
Feelings of emotions will cast your existence away
You can choose to move on or to live repeatedly in the same day
To feel alive again or to live in grey
When you are living on your last memories
You will be trapped in a place of confusion,
Denying your pain and not facing your story
It will leave you lingering in life's unbearable miseries.

A Poem from a Girl

I am pure
But I also seek your words for a cure

We may argue day in and out
But don't deny it; you know what it's all about!

I try to be kind
Giving you piece of mind

Maybe if you'd listen
You'd know by now what's missing

I'm not looking for the perfect man
Cause I'm not the perfect woman

One thing I know for sure
Is that you make me pure

Your love is unexplainable
Making me feel incredible

I appreciate all the things you do
And understand your point of view

But do have an open eye
And see that I also try

Paul Her

What I want is just *YOU AND ME*
And no other lady

So that we can be
Living our wildest fantasies

To be with you
Makes my dream come true

I hope by now you understand
It's time to put this relationship on a win.

WRONGFUL LOVE

Do not be drunken in the moment of desperation, old friend
Love because you choose to love
Not because you need to love in the battle of loneliness
Only a fool will ride the wheels of emotions
A wise person sees the troubles in desperate companionships
Seek not to fall for a person in the times of need
But fall freely for this person when you want true love
Do not be blinded by the physical attributes
My dear friend, being alone is better
Than being lonely with the wrong person.

Paul Her

SHE IS BROKEN

She finally shut her heart
And turned the other way.
Not looking back,
Not thinking,
Wondering *what if…*

She walked away
Not a single peek
Or a question was asked –
Silence filled the melancholic air.

A cold and baleful heart was left behind
She never looked at love the same anymore
Nor did she believe in forever

It is no longer her refuge
Or resting ground.

There, she hastily buried love,
Dishonesty, and shattered pieces from
Her broken dreams.

She hated him.
She yearned for him.
Yet, with a kiss goodbye

She shut the broken door tight
And left out of his sight –For good.

The Deceitful Followers

This contagious, diseased air brushes the innocent souls
Waking the untapped spirits of premature, blossoming creatures
They do not know what they cannot see
Only to survive against the tyranny of time,
Only to follow tainted hope
It is the only way it was displayed to them

The wrong message becomes the just motive
Wicked leaders feeding false hope to naïve dreamers
Preaching hate instead of love, waging war instead of peace
Power outweighs the value of humanity; humility is at its low
Greed is hidden behind every purpose of conflict

Lives are traded for pride
Religions are misguided for radical reasoning
The deceitful followers are misinformed
The world is staged into a deadly Coliseum
It is a dire time, sensitivity at its high,
And selfish pride can ignite explosions

Ebola used for distractions from the real deadly epidemic
Wars in the Middle East will never stop
The puppet masters are to blame, not the murderers
For they only seek peace through false promises
Negotiations are no longer needed, vengeance is priority

Beliefs are more important than flesh
Sacrifices are made for the wrong reasons

Paul Her

Our actions will damage stability,
Will cripple the life-line of mankind
The ending of diplomacy is near, stubbornness is foolishness
Remember –
Nature does not need humans, humans needs nature!

Hate is easily instilled, love is difficult to grasp
But when love becomes contagious it will bring trust and peace.

It Was a Simpler Time

It was a simpler time without demands
Living only to fill your voids,
Not to the standards of social media.
And the standards of society were low,
Not because they had no ambition,
But due to the lack of knowledge they shared.

It was a simpler time without judgments
The universe was yet unknown,
But the earth was an agricultural Eden.
Decorated with nature's beauty.
It was a time at ease, only to live in peace.
Greed was not a factor, hate was living in its fetus.

It was a simpler time without cyber spaces
Living in the present, enjoying the water running down the river
Time was not controlled by hourly wages
Labor was done by choice not by demand
The days were long, but relaxing
There was no pressure to build wasteful monster pyramids

It was a simpler time without deep corruptions
Belonging to yourself, not being owned by governments
Bureaucrats were not poisoned by corporations
Nature was at its finest,
Natural resources were abundant
Now, the world is polluted with lethal human waste

Paul Her

It was a simpler time without broadcast negativities
It was a simpler time; it was a time of respect for all life forms.
It was a simpler time.

The Art of Thoughts

Paul Her

MY DEAR COUSIN

Whilst at your funeral I mourned sadly
I knew I could see myself lying in your place
The crowd was smiling although some cried
There were no tears coming down my face
Was it wrong? I was numbed, stone cold-hearted
But still, I felt I needed to be embraced
Strangers amongst gathered to see you sleeping forever
I wanted to yell, "Please give him some space."
Although I knew you couldn't hear
I knew your spirit was there at the same place
It goes to tell, you were loved
And all your memories brought beauty and grace
Your last days were celebrated like a remembrance of a King
Bringing loved ones from everywhere, even unknown faces
It is the last time I will see you, still I won't cry
But I know, in my heart, you will never be erased.

SHE IS MY BEAUTIFUL

There, she moves swiftly against the breeze
Into the deep hues of *Spring*
Yet, she is the most colorful of all
With sophisticated floral essence
She is my fragrance of love

O she stands perfectly sturdy
Against the harsh, careless wind
My crystalline floral in the garden of love
No toxic fumes can wither away her petals
For I will be her protector from above

There, she lies graceful with unique aroma
Exhibits, proudly, her magnificent strength
Never defeated by any storm
She blossoms as spring gives life once more
Shaken by her beauty, my heart is feeling warm

Paul Her

The Movie of My Life

In me I've always had these *Great* EXPECTATIONS
But I've felt that I'm running OUT OF TIME
I want to aim for PRIDE AND GLORY
To pursue and live in the AMERICAN DREAMZ
Sometimes, I'll be lost and RUNNING SCARED
Consumed in guilt, I'd play the DEVIL'S ADVOCATE
I know I'll feel the WRATH OF THE TITANS
I'm afraid of THE KILLER INSIDE ME
At times, I'm alone like *A MAN APART*
Still in humanity, I see *A FEW GOOD MEN*
Even I know, the strongest can fall like the WORLD TRADE CENTER
I believe in my abilities, I don't have any DOUBT
I will continue to be fearless like *KING KONG*
Waiting for the time to conquer the *EMPIRE*
Until that day, I'll just cherish the *air i breathe.*

A Night Visionary

As I breathe life into my beating heart
Listening to the distractions of temptation
I begin to pull my mind apart
From the wicked human creation

As night grows darker with silence
I stand alone pacing steadily
Listening to the sound of unknown violence
Waiting to craft my finest masterpiece

As I work with the choice to unveil my thoughts
I brush my words gently like a Chinese Calligrapher
Expressing my most sacred piece of art
For many, I'm wasting my time, for some I'm changing their futures

As I put the finishing touch on my unheard sonnets
I write the final words to impact lives
In hope – it will strike many like a comet
Teaching valuable lessons, giving way to strife

Paul Her

OH, MR. GATSBY

Oh, Mr. Gatsby, your love for her is uncandid
Unparalleled, beyond that of a mortal
Oh, Mr. Gatsby, your love is foolish
But why do I admire your commitment?
It is unusual; it is not of me.
Still – I am impressed by your unconditional love
The measure of your heart
Not of human characteristics, deep rooted.
Oh, Mr. Gatsby, your love is full of stupidity
But, of purity and conviction
Though, not an act of nobility,
I can truly comprehend your intentions
You walk in depth of sins
However, you live life with dignity
Oh, Mr. Gatsby, you died for love
And I am prideful, a bit stubborn
Yet, I believe I will die too.

Gone, but not Forgotten

The best ones will not reach the full extent of life
It is not meant to be; it is the will of God
He wants us to remember them at their best
Not at their worst; it is a lesson to all sinners

When they are gone, they are not forgotten
For they have displayed life's beauty
Through them, we gain grace and sincerity
For us, it teaches not to take life for granted

The young ones are taken too soon
To remind the world to love each other fully
The earth has lost its saints,
But heaven has gained angels

When they are gone, they are not forgotten
Life is full of tragedies; life may be rough
Be sweet mourners, never give up
Live the best of your days; live for something

Paul Her

SELFISH HEARTS

They possess stone-cold, frozen hearts.
Each stubborn soul as solid as a rock, yearning to part.
No words pass through their aggressive ears.
Silence of deep tension, filling thin air.

The feeling of hate and revenge pushed to the boiling point.
Their pain and fear growing stronger
And louder as their hopes would disappoint.
No more love remains in their cold, frozen, white hearts.
And soon, evil will tear them –
Death apart.

INCARCERATION

I weep quietly without tears
My heart is crying inside my congested chest
Surrounded by love, but I'm still in fear
My loneliness won't let go of my past
All my mistakes cannot make up for those missing years
I'm praying for my bad karma to pass
I wish for all of us to be here
And I want this moment to last

You guys are grown; I am proud
My heart is crying when it's time for you to go
This day forward I am making a vow
As a strong father I won't let my struggles show
I will take care of you all, starting now
And give the best love until I grow old
My crying heart is beating a little slower
I will rest now; I can finally sleep on top of the clouds.

GREED OF HUMANITY

The human appetite
overindulge the three course meal of life,
never satisfied by the delightful
taste of forbidden herbs.
And the tangible ingredients
of erotic flavors.
It will consume all in its way.
Giving no mercy or sympathy.
The human aura never steps aside
for the day.
As night comes,
its hunger grows bigger.
Forever, the human carcass
will not be ashamed.
Only the soul is left.
Lost in the life after.

The Art of Thoughts

Paul Her

My Closest Friends

I've tried so hard to laugh it off,
To find satisfaction in the face of love.
Travelling from the east to the west,
To watch life's comedy show at its best.
I search for music to soothe my soul,
But the song of sadness won't let me go.
I dig for gold to bring happiness,
Even the heart is not satisfied with riches.
The true genuine smile is far,
Farther from the truth, afar from the stars.
'Til I reached the end of my destiny,
I came to see.
All the laughter I need
Lies in the hands
Of my closest friends.

DEAREST...

Dearest my stubborn self,
Why do I stay so prideful?

Dearest my temperamental self,
How did I get this awful?

Dearest my sensitive self,
Why do I allow hurtful words to overcome?

Dearest my ungrateful self,
How did I become so numb?

Dearest my overachieving self,
When will I please myself with contentment?

Paul Her

My Unborn Child

I am not a man of power, only a man of principles
I live to be the best, not to prove a point
But to conquer my fear, I do not wait for miracles
I face the truth without hidden lies
Dear my unborn child, I am not invincible
I have cried, I have lied, and I have failed
But I am not one to give up; it is not medicinal
Against the broken seasons of torture
I have lost my ways, but I am transitional
If you find that life is difficult, do not be afraid
Believe in your ability; be original
The wine of life can be bitter
Let the sunshine nourish love; it is nutritional
Dear my unborn child, life is a steep waterfall of unpredictability
Be not stiff like a wooden pole; be flexible
Like a bamboo tree bending against the monstrous winds
When the storms pass, you will become mythical
It is you against the world at times; it is part of life
My advice – never drown in pity
No one will feel sorry for you; do the unthinkable
Sweep the dust off your troubled house
Reach for the stars; this is your pinnacle.

INNER STRENGTH OF DAVID

I feel like a stranger amongst friends
In the desert of flooded flatlands.
Lost without a star for guidance,
As if the night is a devastating tyrant.
Why am I a lamb amongst lions?
Fighting a lost battle to live in hope of triumph.
Let me pray for my father's keeper;
Giveth the strength of Spartacus to be my protector.
How can I overcome the depressed antics of men?
Is my tribulation part of God's plan?
I will reach for the David in me to fight
Against Goliath and claim my obligated rights.
I can proclaim the strength in me when I believe
Amongst strangers we will become friends in the distant sea.

A Passage in My Mind

The love we give to others
Is the only love truly worth sharing
The only thing we keep
Is the words we speak

The feelings we show
Are to encourage others to care
The promise we make to others
Is the only promise we keep

The hugs we give away
Are to display human decency
The love we give ourselves
Is the only love we seek

O Darlin' Night

O darlin' night, O so ever peaceful
O quiet night, O so ever solely
Your trail of winds is so cold,
Brushing against my tender, yellow face.
So magical
So bold.

O lonely night, O so ever darken
O mysterious night, O so ever blindly
Your movement casts no shadows
Wherever has the moonlight gone?
No sound I hear,
But the whispering wind.

O darlin' night, O so ever refreshing
O mighty night, O so ever powerful
Your spell upon the world
Has silenced the dreamers
Without a sight
Yet, my vision still sees pure beauty.

O everlasting night, O so ever lovely
O darlin' night, my darlin' night.
Go gently into the silent night.

Paul Her

Seasons

In *March* when the smell of blooming flowers
Arise to full aroma,
The green island comes to life from *Spring* showers.
The chirping birds sing of love songs,
Waking creatures, fully hibernated, rise from their comas.
From a lonely, bitter winter, the trees stay strong,
Their naked bark is now covered with leaves
Preparing for the summer, fully sprung.
In *June* when the sun rises early in dawn,
And heat waves surf *Summer* days long,
The golden glare burns lightly in the clear sky.
Its atmosphere keeps calm as the air rests,
While a feast is in ruins by the swarming flies.
When *September* arrives with its fierce wind,
Fall becomes a trendy dress up theme.
With mild temperatures, the colorful trees
Preparing for Halloween.
Children buried under fallen leaves,
Enjoying the last of nature before a freeze.
Before the falling white crystal shower,
We begin family traditions for Thanksgiving.
Feasting like bears before the eve of *December*,
We now feel the cold breeze, soon it will be *Winter*.
And snow angels will come alive by
The lovely children
Who have so much to give to the frozen world.
It is a short moment before long;
The seasons will begin –
And again
With a lonely song.

A United Family

Through the struggles we cry
Against the time we learn
The love from our family makes us smile
With respect, loyalty we earn
Accept our differences and jealousy will burn
Stop the envy and demolish our egotistical pride
Believe in forgiveness
Believe in all of us
We will rise above
With unselfish love.

A Wishful Want

I want to be the world you live in
I want to be where you begin and how you end

I want to be your only destiny
I want to be your eyes to see

I want to kiss you ever lastly
I want to love you faithfully

I want to be the protector of your sea
I want to be the pure blood you bleed

I want to be the oxygen running through your lungs
I want to be your right from your wrong

Paul Her

ANY GIVEN DAY

It asks for no particular name
At any moment it can strike
Regardless of who you are
You can be poor
You can be rich
It will not ask for your approval.
Even Kings of Kings will not be spared,
O it searches no specific face
It will not pick a certain race
No one will see it coming.
It disgusts me!
Many hearts have been broken,
Many good souls have been taken.
If you fight,
You may win
Have faith!
If you are up against it,
Do not be afraid.
It is easy to give up
But always know
It can take your physical appearance
It can take your strength
But it cannot touch your mind,
It cannot touch your soul.
It is harsh,
No warnings will be given,
Have faith; always have faith.

HMOOB CAUBFAB
(HMONG IN THE JUNGLE)

My people of displacement, of hunger
They are torn by Wars
Chased by the Communist Party
Captured, killed, and slaughtered like animals.
For those who escaped and survived,
My heart aches for them, my tears –
I shed many tears for their sufferings.
No hope for tomorrow, diminished dreams
Only to live to survive the day.
They live to wait for General Vang Pao
But after 40 years, the General is dead.
What can they do to find peace?
I see their cries for help with hurting tears,
Their pleas for safety,
And their desperations for food.
Oh I wish for their freedom, but freedom isn't free.
How do we stand together to get them out of harm's way?
They are abandoned by all Communist Regimes
Including their own people, especially us HMONG in the
United States.
They live fearfully with no help in the Jungles of Southeast Asia
Hoping one day they will find peace, but peace is nowhere near.
They cannot live this way; they will not survive being suppressed
like caged animals.
Their stories will be heard
Their lives matter, but will there be enough time to rescue them?
For those who care

Feel the torment of these innocent Hmong left behind by a broken promise
No one is coming back to help and they should know the truth.
Let their dreams die like the death of Unity
May their souls rest in peace and may they be
Reborn as the most prosperous Hmong in the next life.
They are the real heroes, they didn't surrender,
And they refuse to lose to Communist ideology.
They will not bow down to the dictator of genocide
Their identity, their heritage, and their culture are worth losing their lives.
To those who sacrificed – peace be with you (Hmoob Caubfab).

TO MY AMICABLE HMONG WOMEN

It is a true story of these phenomenal Hmong women
They are perfect displays of courage and commitment
Born to serve the macho-obsessed, egotistical men
Without any boundaries, they endure the torment
They leave their own blood family to become members of their husband's family
Even if sometimes they are to be forced into marriage
They do not have a choice; it is the tradition of the Hmong
Once they leave their homes, they are not welcome back,
Forever forbidden from their own clan name; it is harsh
But they are my amicable Hmong Women
They love boldly with discipline and strength
Bravery and loyalty are in their blood
For some, they were left to be the mothers and fathers
The wars took away many fathers
Some sons are gone too soon
My Hmong women, you are brave as brave can be
Protecting the family name without selfish reasons
You stay loyal without him even if he can't see
Oh my amicable Hmong women, you are my Goddesses
I praise you all, I cherish your integrity and values
Some of you may even be married as second or third wife
There are no complaints, most faithful women I know
Although many are mistreated by sexism among Hmong society
These women stand proud, never allowing words to defeat them
The road you take is less travelled
My beautiful Hmong women, my amicable Hmong women.

Paul Her

LOVE AND JUSTICE

Pass through times gracefully
With intent to love peacefully
Give to those who are unfortunate
And show pure passion if you are fortunate

Share without being acknowledged
Help to give the weak courage
Perform kindness to all humanity
Abolish racism and untasteful cruelty

Defend those who are victims of injustice
Bring forth the fairness of the righteous
Display love without judgement
Unite together; fight against racial resentment.

Hurting Inside Me

When I heard the bad news, I refused…
Is this real… why do I have to always lose?
It's been a few days, I'm confused…
I am broken knowing this wouldn't last, I thought life was smooth.
It is not fair for us, shed me some tears from above
Sorry for my selfishness, I am clearly lost
We came a long way, from friends to this bond of love
It's been a lonely day without you. God… why this loss?
Who would have predicted this heartache?
The confusion and pain on my face
Shows the hurting during this slow phase
I remember all the good days we have been through
From the hard work to being a great crew
I will be hurting for a while without you my friend
But I will tell you everything when we meet again
You are in a better place now
Looking back on our memories; I am so proud.

Paul Her

Who Do We Blame?

In today's society, I see many issues
I see cops killing black teens
I see women doped up like twisted fiends
Hooking in motels and hotels, making a living
Broken Liberty, unfair justice system
A white child molester gets 5 to 10 years in prison
While black teachers face racketeering charges
Up to 20 years in our justice system
For what? For cheating…
Who do we blame for these messes?
Our President is black and the racism might seem less
But in this nation only the upper class are blessed
The state of Missouri deployed the National Guards
Rep. John Lewis called on Obama to declare Marshall Law
In Ferguson we witnessed the new revolution
We are the "Home of the Brave"
The wealthiest nation, but for health care we have no solution
We can say goodbye to social security
Even our own government doesn't trust our Homeland Security
A country known for being "The land of the free"
Shit, nothing here is free, more like modern slavery
Who is to blame for bigotry?
Gay rights is in full blossom
But Alabama said it is not of their customs
Indiana said it is against their religion…
How can we be free?
When the elitists are mandating our destiny
And abusing democracy and jailing many helpless beings.

BROKEN DREAMS

They say the best is yet to come
And for those who are wise to be patient
Yet, in order to succeed you have to fail
Numerous times on many occasions
Mistakes are made to be forgiven
Opportunities come in many forms
The path of failure is a blessing,
Even in the wake of broken dreams
Experience is an important lesson
If you want something
Reach out to grab it and search
For a shining star in the dark sky
Many believe losing is a curse
But I believe it to be the teacher of life
When people strive through strife
There are no broken dreams
The only way to succeed and win
Is to redeem your own self-esteem

Paul Her

I Am Free (My Soul)

If I die not because of my stupidity, I will be satisfied
If a harsh disease chooses to consume me
I will die purely, I am not afraid, I will not lie
When the body suffers, the soul is free

I will gladly meet my match when my time is due
I will not give in to the test of misery
I will no longer worry; I am free
Go – go gracefully but I won't take the plea

I will fight until my last breath
And if you know me, I will not stand to be silent
But when it's time I'll take my rest
Within each breath, peace conquers violence

The Art of Thoughts

A Secret Garden

From the outside I saw you many times
Never did I intend to stop by
I must admit I was judging with blurry eyes
Blindly, the swamp of the jungle lies
With hidden beauty it speaks to me
Whispering endless imagery for my eyes to see

In a place of no colors
I can see a secret garden full of flowers
It gives life to me once more
I embrace the raindrops as it pours
I hide under the sheltered trees
As nature's powerful force roams free
I stand to adore
Wishing for this secret garden to soar
And show its glittering glare
Like the most radiant star of stars
For all to see your refined beauty from afar

Paul Her

Mishap of Time

When the time comes calling,
No amount of treasure can purchase
Your next breath.
Nothing in the world can stop
This force of wickedness.
All the money from the royal palace
Cannot amount to your priceless existence.
Do not wait until this last moment
To seize for more time,
For it will be a result in
Which you will greatly be disappointed.

Paul Her

When I Am Gone

When that day comes and I am gone
Do not weep for me
I am strong.
This day –
I did not choose,
Nor does it belong to me.
Remember me for the way I smile,
Picture me like the wide sea
Long gone into the silent miles
I will vanish into the dark, cold, lonely night.
Remember me through the stars when they shine bright
Remember my shadow from the sunlight
Remember my presence in the moonlight
Do not be sad,
Most likely, I'm leaving on destiny's flight.

Hate Hinders

Why do we call this horrendous thing hate?
Is hate the act of misunderstood love?
I say hate is created by man to halt progression
In human evolution.
I say hate is the ultimate crime
We only choose to hate because
We believe hate hiders time.
What is the purpose of hatred?
Are we born to hate? It is instilled in our DNA?
I say we must learn to accept the truth
If we see our own faults
And take full responsibility to fix our mistakes
Instead of blaming others,
We can learn to love.
Hate hinders the future of our children
But love and peace will bring togetherness
Around the world.

Paul Her

Lion's Entrapment

"There are two lions inside us
waiting to come out,"
said the Wiseman to his son.
"One is ugly, hateful, envious, evil,
pretentious, tooth-faced, and selfish.
One is beautiful, faithful, good-spirited,
giving, loving, and nice.
Only one of them can win."

"Which one of them will win?,"
asked the young curious man.
The Wiseman waited for a moment
and replied, "Son, the lion who wins
will be the one you choose to feed."

THE CONCEPT OF GOOD

In life a good person will never take
Credit for the goodness he does.
He will not boast about the possessions which
He has acquired.
Many times he will be put down
But he will not fight with words
He will only demonstrate with his heart.
Even when he gets criticized, embarrassed, or denied
For his effort of good deeds,
He will not listen to negativity.
His eyes are on the prize
And his only focus is to reach his goal.
But he will not display greed along the way.
Good spirit and generosity
Will be given to the people he touches.
The amount of money and possessions
Will not define his success,
Rather, the life he leads
Will tell the story of his success.
He will live life
Instead of letting life live him.
He performs good for what he believes,
Not for acceptance.
In his heart, it is young
He knows no hate.
When love is instilled
Hate will not flourish.
Give him all the lessons

Paul Her

To be ashamed of hatred
And good will tarnish all evil
In this lost world.

ALONG THE ROADS

I travel the road
To seek the undiscovered beauty
Sometimes when I feel skeptical
I stay unafraid, unshaken
For I will experience the different cultures
I will see the different stages of life

Along the way
I will meet many people
They will share their stories
And their insightful words
It will inspire my inner-being

To learn what life
Can offer
Will exhibit the uniqueness
Of humanity; in the process of adaptation
I will ask the unanswered questions
Because no answer is as good
As the truth from local wise men

I travel the road
Not to collect the dust
But to find the ugly truth
Which is concealed
From the world to see
The people around the world
Deserve to know the reality of suffering

Paul Her

But life is beautiful
Full of hypocrisy,
Full of lies,
And filled with happy sorrows.
Just travel the roads
And it will lead you to the land of happiness.

HER CRY FOR HELP

She said, "Can you sing me a love song
to cure my lonely heart?"
So I did,
I sang her a love lullaby with a harmonious tune
As tender as the voice of Elvis Presley.
Then she said,
"Can you sing me a sad song so I can cry
away all my wrongs?"
So I did,
I sang her a verse with the sound
Of soft, heavenly, harp melodies,
Sending a sad vibration through her soul.
Then she asked,
"Can you whisper some words into my ears to
make me smile radiantly."
So I said,
"If God is real, I'd believe you are
His most perfect creation."
Before she closed her eyes
To fall asleep, she smiled beautifully
And asked for one last favor.
She said, "Can you sing me a sweet, slow
song to send me to Wonderland?"
And I did,
I sang her an *A Capella* with sweet rhyme filled
With the smooth harmony of Barry White
Which hypnotized her into a tranced state of mind.
And so she rested with a smile of an angel
Until the morning sunrise.

Paul Her

A Mother's Love

She loves unconditionally without
Any love in return
She gives her heart to us
Without being earned
She is unselfish without any
Hesitation to die for her children
Even when she is hurt, she won't cry
She stays strong for us
Even when we can see the hurt in her eyes
A mother's love is unmatched,
Unlimited, as wide as the ocean of skies
Without our dear mothers, this world
Would be a depressing sunrise.

An Introduction into My Perspectives

Words for Thoughts

Those who teach hatred will receive threefold
the magnitude of hate.

It is very difficult for decent men to prevail
during indecent times.

Humans are not perfect, but in the quest for
finding perfection, they can learn to be great.

A few of us will live life to find the truth,
but most of us will live life blindly in lies.

He who is pure with his intentions does
goodness with his actions.

Be wise; ignorance is the ultimate
characteristic of failure.

Paul Her

Quotes for Insights

Live each day as your last,
for tomorrow may never get here.

There is no division in any family. What I see
are people who choose to divide themselves from others.

Behind every happy face lies a story
of sadness.

In your circle of trust,
don't trust the complete circle.

Don't open your kingdom to someone who doesn't
appreciate your peace and happiness.

Don't open your heart
to someone who is heartless.

A Simple Truth

If you ask me a simple question about life,
I will give you a direct answer on the
way I live my life.
If you want to know what life means to me,
I will only give you an answer about
the way I see life.
Many of us will never get to see the bright light,
But as long as we try to give our best,
we will never regret not seeing the light.
In life, as long as we've done our best,
it doesn't matter what we get out of it,
We will be content without any regret.
I can't guarantee anyone any promise,
but if I give you my word,
I will not let you down.
If you are always expecting something in return,
chances are, you will be disappointed.
In the truth, live your life for yourself,
not for others.
If you are living to satisfy others,
you will never find happiness.

VIEWS ON ISOLATION

In solidarity, the inner-truth
is found in one's character.

Isolation is the key to
embracing the true self.

Being alone is not a bad thing.
It is a thing of beauty.
One can really put in the
time to seek for self-knowledge.

It is when you are alone
that you understand to love yourself.

At the end of the day.
You realize in solitude.
There is only me, myself, and I.
No others will stand by you.

Isolation strengthens your ability
to appreciate the valuable people
in your life.

Views on Mindfulness

No personality, any more than the earth,
can sustain its originality.

If we are overly prejudiced, we are too naïve
to understand the differences in mankind.

Work for a better today;
hope for a safer tomorrow.

A man is only as good as his words.

A fool is a person who thinks of others as fools.

When we have no more emotions,
we will soon give way to death.

Patience is a virtue,
but patience cannot be procrastinated.

VIEWS ON MEASUREMENT OF LIFE

Happiness is not defined by money, success, or power,
rather is it measured by the state of mind of each individual.

Don't measure me by my achievements
or my status in life; measure me by my willingness
to treat others equally.

Life is not defined by how big your bank account is,
it is measured by how big your heart is.

A true champion is not defined by the number of wins,
but measured by the amount of wins
within quality competitions.

My life should be measured by the number
of people I have affected and touched.
I should only be worth as much as
the positive influence I have had upon people.

The strength of a man is not measured
by his physical size,
rather it is determined by
the size of his will.

Being Afraid

Most people are afraid of popular opinion.
They are afraid to be wrong, to be criticized,
or to be an outcast.
In contrary, I am not afraid of being wrong.
In fact, most of the time I wish I was wrong
because if I am mostly wrong, the world
is a better place.
If I am right it means that obvious
things are happening. It is not good.
Many times I will take a stand on an issue
and sometimes I will form enemies, but
if I can see that my opinion will give truth
I will allow people to dislike me. I don't care
what people think of me because I am no longer their prisoner.
We are all different. We think differently. We speak differently.
We believe differently. We need to accept differently.
If you dislike my perspectives and ideologies
I don't mind, but if you dislike my character
and attempt to dismantle my personality,
you have something coming back to you.
Do not be afraid to be yourself.
Think for you. Learn for you.
Speak for you.
Be not afraid of you.

QUOTES ON SELF-HAPPINESS

To live a fulfilled life,
one must live for a principle and die for a cause.

To be fully satisfied,
you have to be honest and truthful towards yourself.

Don't worry about what people think of you,
worry about what you think of yourself.

Let others judge you, let them criticize you,
let them spread rumors about you;
it will only fuel within you a better person.

The true question is can you accept yourself
at the end of each day without worrying about
how people think of you or what they said about you?

Some people have everything they want
and still are unhappy; some people don't
have anything they need and are the happiest.

Quotes on the Possession of Power

The greatest power is the
power of self-control.

Being powerful is not just about status quo,
but is based on character.

Don't underestimate the power of forgiveness,
it is contagious.

Don't sacrifice your integrity and moral value
for the power of hierarchy.

True power is getting people's attention
without taking any action or making any interaction.

Divine power is only given to men of full purity.

In all great leaders, power wasn't given,
it was earned through trust and courage.

Quotes on the Measure of Success

Don't focus too hard on success,
pay more attention to your value.

Focus on your character more than your reputation;
your character is who you are;
your reputation is what people perceive you to be.

Success is not harvested overnight,
its seeds are sowed through the seasons;
you will reap your fruits of success
when it is ripe.

Success is determination plus many failures
multiplied by focused dedication.

Men who await success are doomed
to be less than mediocre.

Be of a success that does not prove others wrong,
but instead prove yourself of your doubts.

Quotes on Being a Leader

The true effectiveness of a leader is to
lead others into progress rather than perfection.

I find everyone to be capable of leading;
leadership is about interacting with people
and helping each other transform in the process of change.
All humans change; nothing stays the same.

A wise leader should never judge based on
words alone, but on conclusive facts
and undisruptive evidence.

A good leader is a reflection of
his or her legacy.

Great leaders are not extraordinary people,
they are regular people doing extraordinary things.

The best leaders listen more often
than they speak. They think thoroughly before
concluding a solution. They will speak for
those in need of help, and they will learn to
observe their followers in part to become better leaders.

The Art of Thoughts

WORDS FOR IMPROVEMENT

I'm an optimistic person,
but I'm always preparing for failure.

I don't know anyone who
is successful that has never failed.

If you live life like a practice game,
you better arrange your priorities.
Life is made of the World Cup,
the Super Bowl, and the Olympics all in one.
It's time to get your best game face on
and compete for your championship trophies.

No matter what the circumstances,
one should not retaliate with violence.

Mistakes are meant to happen,
but when the same mistakes occur multiple times,
then proper punishment is the only option.

A wise man will never conclude
a book by its cover.

BELIEVE IN YOURSELF

To live life is to find happiness.
Although, some of us will never
achieve true happiness,
we must not give up.
In that pursuit of happiness,
it will be quite a journey of despair and disappointment.
And this journey may turn
into a life-long search.
But, it can be achieved if we believe.
We, in life, should never let anyone
tell us we cannot reach our dreams.
We can do whatever we choose to do,
as long as our goals are reachable
and fall in the boundary of our abilities.
If our goals are not realistic,
we cannot conquer something that we cannot see,
we cannot reach something that we cannot touch,
and honestly we cannot grasp something that doesn't exist.
Believe in yourself,
because no one else will.

Words for the Heart

Love only if you love freely;
do not love by force.

Most of the time, the heart will
defeat the mind.
Because the heart conquers love more strongly.

When one dedicates his or her heart
to a set goal, more than likely
he or she will be successful.

Listen to your heart,
it will speak the truth.

A fragile heart is a loving heart.

The eyes see everything physical,
but the heart sees all that is invisible.

A sound mind and a passionate heart
will lead you to infinite opportunities.

Words for the Mind

The mind is very powerful,
don't let it become a deadly bomb.

To have an open mind,
one must have an open-door policy.
Let the lights shine in and let the
changes take place. Refresh the mind
and clean out the useless information.

Words cannot penetrate the heart,
unless the mind gives the words power.

We should train our minds not to memorize facts,
but instead to prepare us to think freely
without any constraint on our thoughts.

You are not at peace
if you are constantly at war in your mind.

You are not free
if your mind is a prison.

THE MIND IS OUR FREEDOM

We can be poor and have nothing
in our possession.
Yet, in our minds we can be rich
and living in a gorgeous palace.
Our minds are very powerful.
In them, we can live in any place
we want or choose.
Our enemy can take the clothes off our backs,
they can take all the money from our pockets,
but they cannot take the imaginations from our minds.
Within these confined walls,
Inside this place we call our minds,
we can seek refuge.
This is a place we cannot be tortured
abused, or captured.
It is our heaven if we choose to be saved.
We will find freedom
if we are no longer a prisoner of our minds.
At last,
we are at peace
if we allow ourselves to be at peace.

DEATH CEREMONY IN THE HMONG COMMUNITY

Hmong people tend to empathize well with each other during funeral ceremonies. In our community, our people value funerals with great pride. More than often, the worth of a dead person is judged based on how much money the family spends on the cost of the funeral. Furthermore, the amount of money collected from donations per visitor will represent how much this person is loved or missed. This has always bothered me because it seems we value death to a high degree. If we help each other while we are alive as we do for the dead, we could have made tremendous progress in our relationships.

I do not think it is wrong for people to spend more than forty thousand dollars for a funeral, but I do think it is not necessary. In the Hmong community across the United States, funerals are becoming a competition, a bragging right, or a showmanship of wealth inside each particular family. Our elders still think that in death, the better the funeral ceremony, the more luck the family members will receive from the spirits of the dead.

Here, I will provide a few suggestions I will give to my Hmong people regardless of their religion. I do not want to criticize anybody. I do not want to tell anyone how to arrange a funeral ceremony. All I want to emphasize is for us to understand that the dead cannot feel or see the magnificent ceremony we are performing for them. Let's get back to the suggestions.

1) We live in a modern society, and we do not need to open a funeral event for four straight days and for twenty four hours a day.

2) It is more economical to have smaller ceremonies without an all you can eat buffet.
3) This is not a party or a social gathering for people to find dates; it is to mourn, and to show respect for the dead and their immediate family.
4) Minimal alcohol, maybe no alcohol (not an actual celebration).
5) Reputation and pride are not worth sacrificing all your life's financial savings. Money will not bring back the dead.

I hope we, as Hmong people, can come to understand the true meaning of death and funerals. When we come to a clear realization of the concept, *"rest in peace,"* we will improve upon the ways which we conduct funeral ceremonies. This will only happen if we actually realize that a funeral is not about the living, but the dead. We are not saving face, instead we are giving a proper respectful ceremony for this individual for the last time before we lay him or her to sleep forever. From my experiences, most funerals are to impress others, but I think if we are to convince people of this as a caring act, we need to love people more when they are alive than when they are dead. When we are dead, we cannot hear or see the love being given to us. Let's love each other fully the best we can. Therefore, when one of us dies we don't have to go out of our way to make up for lost times; while also trying to be pretentious in front of strangers who don't care about the funeral but are also there to fake their own empathy. A false sympathy in the presence of a peaceful gathering is an act of disgrace. It does not only offend the mourning family, but all who are present to pay their love and respect. When we give up self-desire of all forms, we will destroy the indulgence of selfish fulfillment of unnecessary cravings.

Words for Inspiration

You are only poor
because your mind is not rich.

When I get spoiled enough
I want to share some of my blessings to those who are less
fortunate. I feel I don't deserve all that I've received.

Those who think of themselves as more worthy than others
will soon be less valuable as people realize their true character.

If you don't know yourself
you will truly not understand what you want in life.

We need to realize, we are here to fulfill a purpose.
Our body is just a temple for our soul.
Work wonders in this world, make a change,
and give your all to impact humanity.
Our time is soon forgotten but our foot prints will
lead others to a more prosperous future.

The process of thoughts can be dangerous,
if one uses it incorrectly. Therefore, process your thoughts
positively so you can impact lives with great intentions.

BE AN ACHIEVER IN LIFE

In life, nothing is impossible; the sky is the limit.
In order to achieve throughout life, we must work hard
and have some fortunate luck.
No matter how much you think you can accomplish,
without hard work and dedication you will fail.
You have to give one hundred percent effort
and have some luck to reach your mission.
Without luck it is not impossible,
but it will be tougher.
I believe there are three major elements
which will create a successful goal.
The first element is believing. It is important
because without believing, there is no achieving. When
we believe in something, we start to focus with
determination on precise missions and set goals to reach the finish line.
The second element is hard work. When you are working hard,
you will never give up. You will stay on the path no matter
how bumpy the roads may be or how much trouble it causes;
you will find your balance and continue on with your dreams.
The third element is having luck. This consists of
having the right timing (being at the right place at the right time).
And also,
when you are lucky, opportunities present themselves in many forms.
But do remember,
hard work brings good luck.
Being lucky is not a miracle, it will only
happen if you work hard for it.

WORDS TO REMEMBER

Live life to the fullest, learn from the past,
live in the present, and don't worry about the future.

Knowledge without application is
a wasted possession.

In all the lessons you have learned,
do not focus on the mistakes,
but seek for the wisdom it offers.

The secret to success is
there is no secret, it is plain hard work.

Be a traveler to experience the beauty
of differences, to break regularity, and
to understand the levels of humanity.

The only person to defeat you is yourself.
Fight your fear with hopeful actions.
Create a strong soldier out of *Me, Myself,* and *I.*
Go win the war against failures,
you are now a resilient *General* waiting
to conquer your enemy of self-doubt.

Paul Her

FOR THE LOVE BIRDS

Love is not a game to play;
Such feelings cannot be cured.
A heart is like a piece of fragile glass,
once it is broken, it cannot be put back together.
It can never be constructed to its original form.
It won't be an easy fix.
Even the best sculptor cannot repair it.
When a heart is shattered, its broken love
lingers in the remembrance of betrayal.

Love cannot be judged because it gives the truth.
From the truth, the evidence is presented by sensational feelings.
Love is pure because it is innocent.
It should never be forced, rather it should be found.
If love is meant to be, "let it be."
Let love be discovered, leave it to "chances,"
when it is least expected, it is true love.

Have faith in love.
If you fall in love, do not resist.
Love is not just for a moment, love is a lifetime commitment.
With love, we can survive through
any torture or suffering.
For love, we can live through pain.

Without love, we will die even
with all the riches in the world.